Forest Family

An Illustrated ECK Parable

by Harold Klemp

Forest Family: An Illustrated ECK Parable
Copyright © 2010 ECKANKAR

All rights reserved. No part of this book may be reproduced, stored in a retrieval system, or transmitted in any form by any means, whether electronic, mechanical, photocopying, recording, or otherwise, without prior written permission of Eckankar.

The terms ECKANKAR, ECK, EK, MAHANTA, SOUL TRAVEL, and VAIRAGI, among others, are trademarks of ECKANKAR, PO Box 2000, Chanhassen, MN 55317-2000 USA.

100318a

Printed in USA
Text from *Stories to Help You See God in Your Life*, ECK Parables, Book 4, by Harold Klemp
Illustrated by Amanda Gunz
Edited by Patrick Carroll, Joan Klemp, and Anthony Moore

Library of Congress Cataloging-in-Publication Data

Klemp, Harold.
   Forest family : an illustrated ECK parable / by Harold Klemp.
      p. cm.
   "Text from Stories to help you see God in your life"—T.p. verso.
   ISBN 978-1-57043-333-7 (pbk. : alk. paper) 1. Spiritual life—Eckankar (Organization) 2. Eckankar (Organization)—Doctrines. 3. Parables. I. Klemp, Harold. Stories to help you see God in your life. II. Eckankar (Organization) III. Title.
   BP605.E3K5545 2010
   299'.93—dc22
                                      2010034303

∞ This paper meets the requirements of ANSI/NISO Z39.48-1992 (Permanence of Paper).

Our backyard feeder attracts a community of animals.
Besides birds we have raccoons, squirrels, rabbits, chipmunks, and deer.

We call the rabbit Stretch. He is very cautious when he comes up to the feed dish, day or night. His only defense is his speed. Fear keeps him alive, and he's grown to be big and old.

Some say the rabbit is a symbol of fear and the deer is a symbol of gentleness. The other day a beautiful doe and a six-point buck came to the feed dishes. I heard a crash in the brush as they approached. The buck came up to the doe, bumped her out of the way, and stooped to the dish himself.

The rabbit sat opposite the dish, watching the buck.
They were only four or five feet apart. I was proud of the rabbit's bravery.
I told my wife, "The deer hasn't learned anything about gentleness,
but the rabbit is learning something about bravery."

The rabbit and squirrels are about equal. Each waits for the other to eat first. If the rabbit's there first, the squirrels get a little pushy and boisterous, but they wait until the rabbit decides to leave the dish.

The most nervy of the creatures is a little chipmunk. He doesn't have any grace at all. When he comes out of the woods, he can hardly see over the top of the grass, but he runs straight at the squirrels. He zips through, coming up behind them, and he scares the living daylights out of them. The squirrels dash up the trees, and the chipmunk flies at the doves next. Pretty soon he's cleared the area and has the dish to himself.

The blue jays are outranked by the squirrels, but they're clever.
They'll start making a lot of noise when the squirrels are at the dish.
"Danger! Danger!" they scream.
And the squirrels all run off into the trees, leaving the dish clear for the blue jays.

This little group makes up a spiritual community.
They're learning their little lessons about when to come to the feed dish.

I look at them and think how much they are like people.
People divide themselves in one way or another, by age, race, religion, or political affiliation.
At the same time they forget we are all God's creatures. What really matters is how people treat each other in the human community.

For Further Reading, Study, and Fun

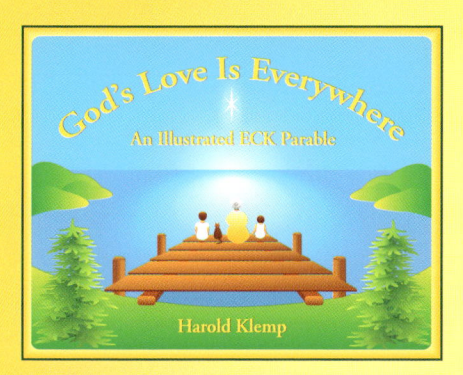

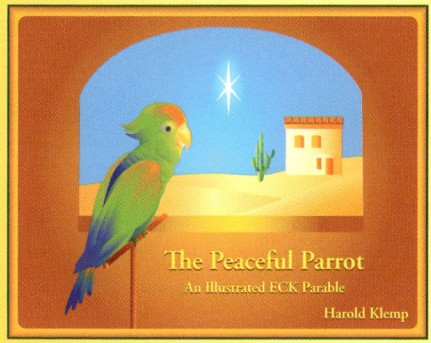

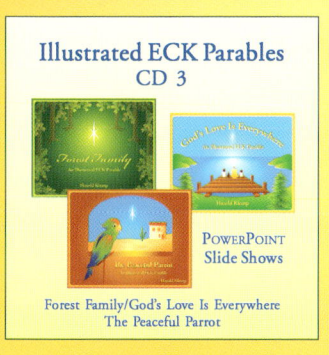

God's Love Is Everywhere
The Peaceful Parrot

Illustrated ECK Parables

by Harold Klemp

Harold Klemp's parables have brought spiritual wisdom and inspiration to seekers everywhere. Now available in beautiful, full-color booklets illustrated by artist Amanda Gunz, these parables will be treasured by youth of all ages.

You have just finished reading *Forest Family*, and two more booklets, shown at left, are waiting for you to enjoy.

Also available is *Illustrated ECK Parables CD 3*, a PowerPoint slide show of these three parables for use in events for youth and families.

Available from Eckankar: www.Eckankar.org; (952) 380-2222; ECKANKAR, Dept. BK94, PO Box 2000, Chanhassen, MN 55317-2000 USA.

More Illustrated ECK Parables

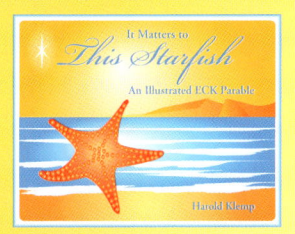

It Matters to This Starfish

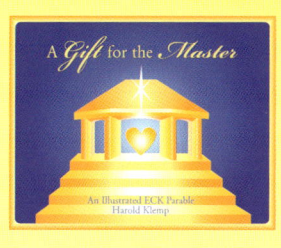

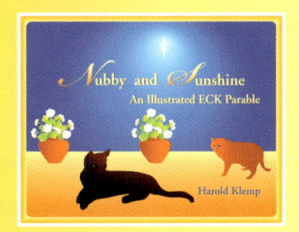

Nubby and Sunshine

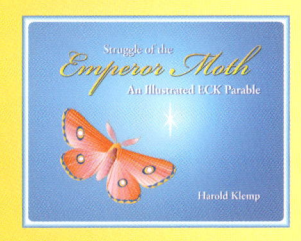

Struggle of the Emperor Moth

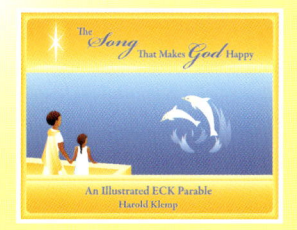

A Gift for the Master

One Small Thing for Love

The Song That Makes God Happy

Illustrated ECK Parables by Harold Klemp

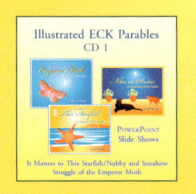

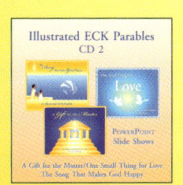

Also available are *Illustrated ECK Parables CD 1* and *Illustrated ECK Parables CD 2*, containing PowerPoint slide shows of these six parables for use in events for youth and families.

Available from Eckankar: www.Eckankar.org; (952) 380-2222; ECKANKAR, Dept. BK94, PO Box 2000, Chanhassen, MN 55317-2000 USA.